This Game

Andria Shook

Illustrated by Steve Pileggi

◦d· **Dominie Press, Inc.**

Publisher: Raymond Yuen
Series Editor: Stanley L. Swartz
Consultant: Adria F. Klein
Editor: Bob Rowland
Designers: Lois Stanfield and Debra Dickerson
Illustrator: Steve Pileggi

First published 1996
New Edition © 2002 Dominie Press, Inc.

All rights reserved. No part of this publication may be reproduced or transmitted in any form or by any means without permission in writing from the publisher. Reproduction of any part of this book, through photocopy, recording, or any electronic or mechanical retrieval system, without the written permission of the publisher, is an infringement of the copyright law.

Published by:

Dominie Press, Inc.

1949 Kellogg Avenue
Carlsbad, California 92008 USA

www.dominie.com

ISBN 1-56270-477-X

Printed in Singapore by PH Productions Pte Ltd
1 2 3 4 5 6 PH 03 02 01

ITP

This game is played
with a red ball.

This game is played
with a white ball.

This game is played
with a brown ball.

This game is played
with a yellow ball.

This game is played
with a black ball.

This game is played
with a blue ball.

This game is played
with an orange ball.

This game is played
with many balls.